LET THE PROPHETS SPEAK

Kevin van der Westhuizen

*This book is dedicated to all those
wonderful saints who will be part of
this great new wave of God.*

LET THE PROPHETS SPEAK

PROPHECY

Your vision shall become new and greater and your borders shall be extended and take you to a place where your borders are wide enough. Lift up your voice unto Me, says the Lord and when you pray and seek My face the anointing shall come upon you, and you have prophesied, but you shall prophesy with a new and greater anointing, and you have had a Word of Knowledge, but you shall stand in the multitude and you shall pick them out and you shall tell them even as the Lord shall show you and your gift shall make room for you and increase your ministry. For I am about to move, says God, and you are part of my move, you are part of my move, you are part of my move. I am God and nothing shall stand in my way, says the Lord.

This was a prophecy spoken over the author's life by Pastor Drummond Thom of Louisville, Kentucky in February 1985 when Drummond visited the author's church.

It must be noted that all of the above prophecy and more has come to pass without the author having to try and bring it to pass.

CONTENTS

LET THE PROPHETS SPEAK

PREFACE

A young spinster living in Cape Town, South Africa, received a "word of prophecy" that she was going to marry a musician within one year of receiving the word. The "prophecy" went on to describe the physical features of the husband-to-be. The prophecy was well received and the lady waited in anticipation for her other half to arrive.

A few months later a young musician who fitted the description joined the church this woman attended. There was great excitement as she saw her "prophecy" begin to materialize before her eyes.

There were a few problems that began to evolve. This musician was 10 years her junior. This would normally not need to be a problem if there was true love between the two involved. He really wanted to befriend this lady, as they had a common music interest, but was not interested in a deeper relationship.

The months rolled into years and the two people concerned never did get together. The heartache and devastation seen in this woman's life was deeply disturbing. All this because of a **prophecy**.

On numerous occasions different ministers have prophesied over my life. Numbers of prophecies have come to pass, several others have not, cannot, and will not come to pass. Many times I have asked the question, WHY? It is because of my own experiences and those I have seen in the lives of others, that I felt motivated to write this book.

There is a great misunderstanding with regard to modern day personal prophecy. We need to bring a balance into the church as prophecy and prophets will be a daily phenomena in today's church.

As you receive a word over your life the question is, Is This a Prophetic Word or a Pathetic Word? We have a responsibility to test the spirits to see if they are of God.

Chapter One

God's Next Move

God has created this life for His glory. All
of life's problems have revolved around man touching the glory of God. God is not going to share His
glory with anybody. When we can grasp this truth,
that all the glory belongs to the Lord, we will avoid
many of the pitfalls we so often fall into. We are
what we are today because of God's grace. We have
not in ourselves been able to do anything in achiev-
ing the successes in life. In God's day there will be
no room for clowns and cowboys. Great ministries
have risen. Many of them started out with the right
motive and attitudes. Many times man has gotten in
the way, and become a god unto himself, building
his own kingdom; thus meddling with God's glory,
and ultimately fallen. The destruction of some min-

istries has been great, and the repercussions of the deeds of these people will roll on for many years to come. New ministries will come, and as they attempt to take the glory that belongs to God for themselves, their end result will be destruction. Our hearts go out to the men who have fallen. Yet out of their situations there is a lesson each of us can learn.

We are presently about to see a new wave of God upon the face of the earth in this next decade. History has shown that when a person or group of persons enter a new flow with God, persecution is imminent. Unfortunately, the greatest persecutors of those who go with the new wave of God, are those who experienced the last move of God. The reason is that most people, after having experienced a move of God, believe that particular move was God's final move. God is not a stagnant God, and as each wave of God breaks on the shores of life, the next wave is already beginning to form. God's final move, whenever that might be, will usher in the return of His Son.

When the church was birthed, as recorded in the book of Acts, there were great signs and wonders done at the hands of the apostles. Untold multitudes of people were ushered into the Kingdom of God.

The church was meeting daily from house to house. According to Ephesians 4:11-16, Jesus set in the church what is known as the five-fold ministry.

Verse 11 *"And He gave some, Apostles; and some, Prophets; and some Pastors and Teachers;*

Verse 12 *"For the perfecting of the saints, for the work of the ministry, for the edifying of the body of Christ:*

Verse 13 *"Till we all come in the unity of the faith, and of the knowledge of the Son of God, unto a perfect man, unto the measure of the stature of the fullness of Christ:*

Verse 14 *"That we henceforth be no more children, tossed to and fro, and carried about with every wind of doctrine, by the sleight of men and cunning craftiness, whereby they lie in wait to deceive;*

Verse 15 *"But speaking the truth in love, may grow up into him in all things, which is the head, even Christ:*

Verse 16 *"From whom the whole body fitly joined together and com-*

pacted by that which every joint supplieth, according to the effectual working in the measure of every part, maketh increase of the body unto the edifying of itself in love.

FIVE-FOLD MINISTRY

APOSTLE

PROPHET

EVANGELIST

PASTOR

TEACHER

APOSTATE FIVE-FOLD MINISTRY

POPE

CARDINAL

ARCHBISHOP

BISHOP

PRIEST

By the year 500 A.D. the five-fold ministry had disappeared from the church. The church was no longer the vibrant growing force it had been, and an apostate five-fold ministry, namely, the Pope, Cardinal, Archbishop, Bishop and Priest became the substitute. For centuries the church moved into what is known as the dark ages. No great moves of God were recorded during this time. God had always kept a remnant of His people who served and loved Him during these periods. Traditionalism set in, its tentacles captivating man in a form of godliness, but the power of God was the missing ingredient.

At a point when the church was possibly at its lowest, a man named Martin Luther made a declaration that shook the entire world. With vibrant gusto he declared: **THE JUST SHALL LIVE BY FAITH**. God breathed life into the church at this time, and a great move of God broke out. The Lutheran Church was berthed from this move. Man then got involved with God's move, and set in motion his own order, rules, structures, and ultimately formed a denomination with patterns that were not in God's divine order and plan. Today, although a massive organization, the Lutheran Church on a whole, is not the powerful, vibrant force it was at its inception. Men touched the glory of God.

The church moved back into a period of lethargy. God raised up two brothers to begin yet another move. As the Wesley brothers proclaimed: O FOR A THOUSAND TONGUES TO SING, MY GREAT REDEEMERS PRAISE, God once again breathed life into the church, and a new wave was berthed. The Wesleyan revival saw some of the greatest outpouring of God's divine power the world had ever known up to that day. God moved mightily, and out of this move was berthed the Methodist Church. However, once again man touched God's glory with his structures, rules, forms, and ceremonies. The results speak for themselves today.

A few years later, God raised up another man by the name of John Calvin to institute a new wave of God. The establishment of the Baptist Church was the product of this move of God. The pattern noted in the previous moves of God occurred in this movement. Many positive things still evolve from this movement today, but it is not the vibrant move it once was.

William and Bradwell Boothe, a father and son team, recognized the needs of the homeless and hungry. As they walked the streets of London, they saw many people inadequately clothed, huddled together in doorways, trying to shelter themselves from the cruel, winter weather. These people were far from having sufficient food to eat, and many had not bathed for long periods of time. They were what, today, we would call street people. William Boothe, inspired by the Holy Spirit, not only saw that there were numerous needs to be met, but also actively and constructively began meeting those needs. He realized that before these people would respond to the gospel message, they had to be cleaned, clothed, housed and fed. So he offered them soup, soap, and salvation. Multitudes were ushered into God's kingdom during this move of God. Out of this move the Salvation Army was founded. As time progressed, man once again got in the way of God's moving power and touched His glory. Man-made structures replaced God's order. Today, on the whole, the Salvation Army does not flow in the intensity as it did in its earlier years.

At the turn of this past century, God began to pour out His Spirit upon all flesh in an unprecedented manner. Almost instantaneously, all over the world groups of people were experiencing another Acts chapter two. From this wave of God came the Pentecostal Movement. Tongue talking, devil chasing, Holy Ghost filled men, women, and children began to fill the churches. Multitudes came to know Christ as Saviour and Lord. Miracles of healing and deliverance began to increase. Signs and wonders were the order of the day. These people were greatly persecuted, not only by the unsaved, but also by the traditionalists. Singing became more vibrant with clapping and dancing in church services becoming a regular occurrence. Great emphasis was placed on the moving of the Holy Spirit and speaking in tongues. A whole lot of Spirit is good, but if we have **all** Spirit, we will blow up. A whole lot of Word is good, but if we have **all** Word, we will dry up.

What we need is a balance of Spirit and Word which will cause us to grow up. The Pentecostal Movement flooded the earth with new revelation knowledge of God's Word. Many Pentecostals believed that the move of God they experienced was the last move of God. Those who thought this were mistaken because a few years later, God moved again. Pencostals, by this time, had also established their form, doctrine, and structure.

The next move of God saw the birth of the Charismatic Revival. This involved a liberated group of people, free from bondage of form, ceremonies, and what they were and were not allowed to wear. God began to shed more light on His Word, and the eyes of the understanding of many were enlightened. Like all others, this group was persecuted by their predecessors. The Charismatic Movement was the fastest growing Movement on the face of the earth. A powerful move of God surged through these people touching and changing the lives of many. This was not God's last move for God moved yet again.

A few years later, a new move of God seemed to flow over the church with dramatic intensity. This was known as the Word Movement. Powerful, Holy Ghost inspired teaching touched the lives of many. The church was taught who they were in Christ, what their rights were, how to clothe themselves with the full armor of God, and many other daily life-giving truths. This, like all the other moves of God was an exciting time for the church. Yet, God is not a stagnant God, and is now ready to move again, ensuring that this, too, was not His final move.

The next move of God which is about to break on the shores of life will possibly be the greatest and most exciting of all previous moves. This move will not be instituted by any single man, group, or organization. The day of the "One Man Show" **is over**. There is only **ONE MAN** who will glory in this move - HIS NAME IS JESUS CHRIST, THE SON OF THE LIVING GOD. As God moves again, it will not be a certain remnant that He will call from any particular group, as has been the pattern in the past. No, this move will include Baptists, Methodists, Catholics, Lutherans, Salvationists, Pentecostals, Charismatics, and every other group or person washed in the precious blood of Jesus who is willing to be caught up in this great move of God. No one man's doctrine will be pre-eminent, but we will be brought into the unity of the Spirit in Faith.

Each group or denomination has received a profound truth from God, and have experienced an authentic move of the Holy Spirit. What we need to realize is that no one group received the full revelation during the time God moved upon them. The revelation received by the Baptists was part of the complete revelation. The revelation received by the Pentecostals was another part of the greater revelation. Each group and move has received a part of the ultimate revelation. Piecing these parts together, plus what God is about to do in this next move, will shed a greater light concerning God's ultimate plan that only now has been realized. Each group has had their doctrinal differences which has resulted in one major occurrence in the church - DIVISION.

And He shall send Jesus Christ, which before was preached unto you: Whom the heaven must receive until the times or RESTORATION of all things, which God has spoken by the mouth of all His holy prophets since the world began (Acts 3:20-21). At this time, as part of the restoration program of God, we are seeing the five-fold ministry being restored. With every move of God, there has always been a fleshly aspect that man has incorporated in the move. Also, there have always been the phonies or counterfeits. God ordained that music be used as the vehicle with which we worship Him. Satan has taken this very God ordained creation, and perverted it for his use. Today, many christians avoid good music because of all the negatives they have seen and experienced with music. Our problems have been that instead of focusing in on all of that which is godly, we tend to focus in on the negatives. With our attention on the negative, we miss out on the blessings that do flow in the things that are godly. We need discernment to know what is of God, and what is not of God. We need to throw out all which is ungodly, and hold on to that which is godly. After bathing a baby, we do not throw the baby out with the dirty water.

Many things will be restored to the church in this next move. This move, among other phenomena that are supernatural will include the following:

1. Divine healing will be replaced with Divine Life. It is better to walk in perfect health than to need to be healed. The greater revelation will supersede the lesser.

2. We will arrive at places before we even leave. Christians will be translated from one place to another just as Philip after having ministered to the Eunuch was translated from the road between Jerusalem and Gaza to Azotus. In this move we will not be seeking the spectacular, but rather the supernatural. I do not come to you with the enticing words of men, but in domination of the spirit and power (1 Cor. 2:4).

3. The power of the spoken word will become a reality. Not a name it, claim it mentality, but a reality of seeing God's word produce. God is a creator and created heaven and earth by the utterance of His word. We will speak to the famine lands of the world to produce.

4. Immediately prior to this move, there will be a separation of the sheep from the goats. Wishy washy, half-hearted Christianity will have no place in this move. Those who are lukewarm will be spewed from His mouth.

5. A mighty harvest of souls will be witnessed during this time. There will be no man-made gimmicks to reap souls, but rather an authentic drawing of the Spirit of God. The world will be moved by the reality in the lives of Christians, and will know that it is the church that has the answers to life.

6. Signs, wonders, and miracles will be the order of the day instead of being isolated incidents.
The Prophets are coming.

7. The Lord will be the only one to receive glory in this time.

This is the time for us to position ourselves in the divine center of this flow of God in order that we might be a part of this great move.

If God is offering fullness, then from us He is demanding emptiness. What needs to come out of our lives in order that the fullness of God might come in? Maybe you would like to pause at this moment, and ask the Holy Spirit to reveal anything and everything that is in your life that would grieve Him, and hinder God's fullness. This is a first class move of God that is coming to this world. We cannot ride first class on economy fare.

The ultimate of all we do must have its roots in God. Christ is coming back for a glorious church, not one that is crippled or hiding in their small corner. When Jesus comes, His bride will be one that has prepared herself for the Groom.

In past times there has been far too much manipulation as people have attempted in the flesh to exercise the gifts of God. Many people have received prayer from others who claim to have received a "Word from God" regarding their situation. Unfortunately, these people leave in the same condition they arrived.

WHAT GOD REVEALS, GOD HEALS!

Chapter Two

God's Plan For Ministry

One ministry gift in the five-fold ministry is no greater than the other. In writing to the Ephesians, Paul says that Christ has set in the church Apostles, Prophets, Evangelists, Pastors, and Teachers. It was never God's intention for any of the five-fold ministry gifts to pass away. The complete five-fold ministry is required for the church to grow to maturity. One of the reasons the church has not yet reached maturity is because the full five-fold ministry has not been operating in the Body as God intended.

The five-fold ministry has been set in the church to equip the saints for the work of the ministry. Without all five ministry gifts, the church and ministry will be off-balance. Each ministry gift has a specific function, and together they should dovetail and flow to the benefit of the Body. The Teacher is the ministry gift to the Body that brings a balance to the church. The Pastor is the love gift set in the church to care for the Body. The Evangelist is the soul reaper. The ministry gift of the Prophet is to give direction to the Body, and the Apostle is the ministry gift that touches all the other ministry gifts.

Apostles	-	Govern
Prophets	-	Guide
Evangelists	-	Gather
Pastors	-	Guard
Teachers	-	Ground

The past few decades has seen God restoring the five-fold ministry to the church. Five-fold ministry carries tremendous responsibility and accountability before God.

During the decade of the 1950's, there was a strong leaning towards evangelism. Many men and women of God were called by God with the express purpose of reaching the lost. During this time, the office of the Evangelist was restored to the church. Prior to this time, there were Evangelists, but they were far and few between. During the fifties, many Evangelists were raised into evangelistic ministry.

Some became well known to men. Others were not so well known to men, but well known to God, doing what they were called to do.

The 1960's saw the restoration of the office of the Pastor. The many thousands of converts brought into the church required care. Many Pastors were in pastoral ministry before the sixties, but it was during this decade that God raised this office to maturity.

The 1970's saw an amazing phenomena as God restored the office of the Teacher back to the church, bringing this office to maturity. Up to this time, much of the church was totally caught up in the Salvation, Healing, and Caring messages. Few people knew who they were in Christ, and what their rights as believers were.

It was during this decade that anointed Teachers of the Word were brought into the foreground. Many of their ministries have continued to positively permeate the church today. This decade saw the believers move in greater realistic realms in God. No longer was it only the Clergy doing the work of the ministry. but the Saints began as they were equipped, to take their rightful place and do the work of the ministry. This move of God set the platform for the 1980's.

Up until this time, the church had felt comfortable with the offices of the Evangelist, Pastor and Teacher. God was ready to move again in His divine plan during the 1980's. Through this decade the office of the Prophet was restored to the church. As with each move of God, with the reality came the counterfeit. With the restoration of the office of the Prophet, came many self-professing prophets who ran around the world proclaiming, instead of a "prophetic word", a pathetic word. This caused many to immediately reject this office because of bad experiences, resulting in a lot of pressure being placed on the Prophet. Many true prophets were rejected along with the false prophets. We as individuals have a responsibility to discern what is of God, and what is not of God. In 1 John 4:1 we are exhorted to test the spirits to see whether they are of God. Rejecting the office of the Prophet will hurt the believer and the church, as in God's plan the Prophet is as important, and as required as the other four ministry gifts in assisting to bring the body to maturity.

Not everybody who prophesies is a Prophet. There is a distinct difference in God's Word between the gift of prophecy, and the office of the Prophet. The gift of prophecy operates in the life of a spirit-filled believer as he yields to the prompting of the

Holy Spirit. The office of the Prophet is set in the Church by Christ only. No man can be promoted by man, or set himself up, into the office of a Prophet. Christ appoints the position, leadership recognizes this position, and the individual operates in the position. The 1990's will see the restoration of the office of the Apostle back to the church. This will then cause the full five-fold ministry to be brought to the point of maturity. The saints will then be perfected for the work of the ministry. They will no more be tossed about with every wind of doctrine. The church will now be able to grow up into Him in all things. The Body will see an increase, and a great awakening will move across the church and unsaved world. This will be a most exciting time as a new breed of believers is being raised up.

Jesus said in Matthew 18:18 that He would build His church, and the gates of hell would not prevail against it. With these new people of destiny, the gates of hell will be under pressure like never before. We will move in, tear down the gates of hell, bind the strong man, and spoil his goods.

The way up in God's Kingdom is the way down. We must decrease in order that Christ can increase. Unless a seed fall to the ground and die, it cannot have life and grow. Those seeking the gifts to gain position and power, will surely fail, but those who seek them to bless others will bear fruit in their season. We are here to build the Kingdom of God, not our own.

In order to flow successfully and accurately in prophetic ministry, we must spend much time in the Word of God and prayer. Reading God's Word is a blessing, but we need to go a step further and study the Word to show ourselves approved unto God, a workman that need not be ashamed, rightly dividing the Word of Truth. God is moving today on the church like never before. Many people in recent times have felt the pressures. Some have thought it all to be satan, but have been mistaken as God said that He would shake everything that could be shaken so that, that which cannot be shaken will remain. The church is in a time of being purged and purified so that the glory of this latter temple shall be greater than that of the former. The world has been looking at the church and asking if this is what they're looking for or do they look for something else. Unfortunately, they have not been to excited about the lives of many in the church because of the fruit that has been produced. The church will now be propelled into a time where the glory, glitter, glamour, and gold will not be the foreground picture of portrayal. It will be a church walking in integrity before God and man, united in the Spirit, and in Faith.

Chapter Three

Stir Up That Gift

Paul exhorted Timothy in 2 Tim. 1:6 to stir up or exercise the gift of God which was in him. Many people are praying that God will give them a gift. The gifts of God are within every spirit-filled believer and it is up to the believer to stir up those gifts. God will not stir them up for you. The more we exercise the gift, the easier it gets for us to flow in that gift as we learn to recognize God's leading. Many times the first time we step out in faith and operate a gift, we are unsure of the results because of the faith element involved, and the risk of the unknown. God would rather have you step out in faith, and make a mistake, than not step out in faith at all. God does not necessarily look at the outward action as much as He would consider the inward motives causing us to react in the way we do. God has allowed us room for mistakes. He is not a celestial killjoy waiting with a big whip for us to step out of line so that He can whip us back into line. All we need to do when we make a mistake is repent, and move in the correct direction.

As we begin to flow in the prophetic gift, we need to take one step at a time. No person gets to the top step of a ladder by taking one huge step. No, we get to the top by climbing step by step. In the same way, begin with the gift of prophecy where you are, with what you have. In the same way that we have to grow physically and spiritually, so we also grow in prophecy. We are encouraged in Rom. 12:6 to prophesy according to the proportion of our faith. The more we stir up and exercise the gift, the more we will grow in that gift. No athlete wins a race without exercise and training. As the athlete's body tunes into his will, his exercises and training become easier and more enjoyable to do. The more we exercise the gift, the easier it gets to have confidence in the God who never fails.

When I was a Pastor in South Africa, there was a man in our church who owned a Fitness Club. One day he suggested that I come down to his club on a regular basis and work out. I decided to take up his offer. On my first visit, he wrote out a training program for me and worked through the program with me. The only thing that he changed for the first session was that he did not want me to put any weight on the bar. I did all the warm up exercises and then went through the program. On a number of occasions, while doing the motions of the training with a weight bar that had no weights on it, I asked him if we could put some weight on the bar. I must admit I was feeling a little awkward, because there were a number of people training with hundreds of pounds of weight hanging from their bars. My trainer refused to let me use any weights that day.

After my first training session, I went home feeling like this was going to be real easy. I liked training that was not going to make me feel like I wanted to die. That evening as I was sitting in my lounge chair, I began to feel some muscles in my body come alive that I did not even know existed. I went to bed and slept soundly. The following morning when I awoke my mind told me to sit up, but my body refused. I was aching all over. Muscles that had not been exercised for years had now been stretched. I could not get out of my bed.

I spoke with my trainer and asked him what I should do about my predicament. His suggestion was what I did not want to hear. He told me to come down to the fitness club and he would ensure that we would fix the problem. When I got there he put me through the exact training I had done the day before. I felt great. All my body needed was a warm up and an exercise. The more I trained, the easier it became.

The same is true with prophecy. As we begin to launch out it causes a stretching in us which is uncomfortable. The more we exercise the gift and push through our fears, the easier it becomes to know the voice of God. Paul said that we were to **exercise** the gift which is in us.

Many have the preconceived idea that when we operate in a vocal gift, the Holy Spirit takes such control of our lives that it is impossible to make a mistake. This is not so, as many times when we flow in a vocal gift, God will only give the idea. It is then required that the individual, under God's inspiration, steps out in faith and creates and builds on that idea. It is a step by step walk of faith.

Never prophesy a Word unless God has given it to you. A person flowing in prophecy should never be placed under pressure to prophesy. Pressure will normally cause the person flowing in the gift to miss God. Many times Prophets are placed under pressure to prophesy because they are Prophets. I heard the story of a Prophet who received a telephone call from an unknown woman who wanted him to tell her where she had mislaid her birth certificate. She expected him to get a word from God on this issue for her as - after all, he was a "Prophet." This is an abuse of the Prophetic ministry, and a person making such a request should either be taught the balance of God's Word on the subject, or failing to receive such teaching, be sternly rebuke.

A person flowing in prophecy should always be open to correction. This gift can so easily be misused. Remaining open to correction, and under the right structures of authority, will be a protection to both those giving the word, and those receiving the word. A person who is not open to correction, has an independent spirit, and needs serious counselling. God has no Lone Rangers. Correction is a God-ordained vehicle to help steer us in the right direction.

1 Cor. 12:11 says that the gifts of the Spirit are divided to every man as the spirit wills. We need to understand that the spirit is willing for us to flow in

the gifts, and as we make ourselves available to be used of Him, He is willing to use us. Paul operated in all nine of the gifts of the spirit. God does not deal the gifts out like someone would deal out a deck of cards, but rather, looks for the available vessel.

What is the best gift? 1 Cor. 12:31 says we are to desire the best gifts. The best gift is the gift I require for the occasion. Should a man be ill, he would not need a word of prophecy, but for him at that time, the gifts of healing would be beneficial.

The ultimate purpose for the manifestation of the spirit is that all who are influenced by this manifestation would profit. God is a Creator, not a destroyer. When prophecy is used to destroy an individual or group of people, IT IS NOT FROM GOD.

Prophecy has always been around. The church let go of this truth and lost the free flow they knew. Satan counterfeited this with people such as gypsies with crystal balls, tarot cards and tea leaves. Now is the time for the Prophets to go in, and repossess the land, and put these ungodly people out of business.

We are exhorted in 1 Cor. 14:1 to desire spiritual gifts, but rather, that we may prophesy. Prophecy is set in the church for a three-fold purpose, namely, edification, exhortation, and comfort. New Testament prophecy is not there to expose all the dirty washing in a person's life. There is a place for this, but that place is not in public. When Jesus asked the woman at the well where her husband was, he continued to tell her she hade five husbands, and the man she was living with was not her husband. Immediately, she recognized Jesus as a Prophet. Had Jesus ministered this to her in a condemning manner, she might have been devastated. Her reaction, after having spoken with Jesus, revealed how blessed she was by the word spoken to her. She went calling all to come meet this man who had told her all about her life. Christ did not openly condemn her, but rather, issued her with the truth of a alternate lifestyle. Prophecy will build faith in the recipient, and will cause them to be blessed, even if it means dealing with negative aspects in their life.

When we prophesy, we edify the church. 1 Cor. 14:31 says we can all prophesy for the purpose that all may learn, and all may be comforted. We need to learn how to exercise the gift, which can be done as we learn how to recognize God's voice.

Prophecy is God speaking to people through people. God always uses a channel through whom He can flow. We are His feet, His hands, His mouth. We are His body. God is looking for an available vessel. God can and does use our ability, but He also goes beyond our ability and uses our availability. Many mighty men of God had little education, almost no ability, but made themselves available to God. He then used them. Prophecy is man or woman speaking, inspired by the Holy Ghost. God will use you as you are. At no point of time do we lose control of what we are doing. The spirits of the prophet are subject to the prophets.

At least three of the following four gifts should be evident in the life of a Prophet, namely the Word of Wisdom, the Word of Knowledge, Discerning of Spirits, and Prophecy. Prophecy will include past, present, and future. Wisdom and the Discerning of Spirits sets a foundation on which the prophecy can then be built.

Chapter Four

Testing Prophecy

In 1 Thessalonians 5:20 Paul urges us not to despise prophesying. Prophecy is the only gift Paul encourages us not to despise. Confusion will cause a person to despise prophecy. A person can receive a word of prophecy, and not understand what God is saying at that particular point in time. A previous unfulfilled prophecy can also cause despising of the gift. It is dangerous to reject all prophecy because of a past negative experience in the same way that it would be unprofitable to the body if we rejected all intercession because of some people acting unwisely in that ministry.

Prophecy must not be used as an ouija board.

When God's Word is used as a "lucky dip" to try to obtain a specific scripture for a specific occasion, some trying results may evolve. It's like the man who asked God for a word, and said that as he opened the Bible, the first scripture he read he'd believe was God speaking to him. His eyes fell on the scripture - "And Judas went and hanged himself." Alarmed, he tried for a second scripture of more encouragement. This time he read - "Go ye and do likewise." Devastated, he made a third attempt and arrived at the scripture that read - "Whatsoever ye do, do hastily." Such abuse of the Word of God could have some critical results God's entire Word must become our life, not just part of our lives.

An opportunity for a negative experience in prophecy, will be available when a person goes seeking a word by asking people to prophesy to them. God can, and will work on our behalf if we should have a desire that He use somebody to confirm a situation to us. As we trust Him He will raise up a prophetic word that can bring joy to our lives. Prophecy should never be used to substitute a lazy prayer or Bible study life.

A person flowing in prophetic ministry must have a sound knowledge of the Word of God. A lack of this knowledge will cause a person to perish. "My people are destroyed for a lack of knowledge" - Hosea 4:6. Knowledge of the Word helps to know that the prophecy is lining up with the Word of God.

All prophecy must be tested. The following points will help to measure all prophecy to test whether it is godly or fleshly.

1. **Prophecy must bring peace**. The Word of God says that we are to let the peace of God rule in our hearts. God's Word to us will <u>always</u> bring peace.

2. **All prophecy must line up with the Word of God**. A prophecy contrary to the Word of God must be immediately rejected. God will never speak anything contrary to His Word. An example of a prophecy that must be rejected would be one where a person receives a word that he is no longer required to tithe to his home church, but should rather tithe to another ministry. Such a prophecy is totally contrary to God's Word. We know the Word teaches clearly that we are to bring all the tithe into the storehouses (our local church.)

3. **All prophecy must bear an inner witness**. If a prophecy does not bear witness when given, do not

reject it immediately as this could be because the individual receiving the prophecy, for many various reasons, has not heard from God. It would be beneficial to seek God concerning such a word. If it continues to fail to bear witness, it would then be safe to store it, and later, maybe, reject it.

4. **Prophecy must come to pass**.

Should a prophecy bear a condition to the fulfillment of that prophecy, and those conditions are not met, the prophecy will not come to pass. This is not the fault of the one prophesying, but rather, due to the disobedience of the recipient. God's Word is full of promises, but many of them are conditional. We all enjoy the promise that says if we resist the devil, he will flee from us. For that promise to be fulfilled, we have to apply the condition which is found in the same verse. The condition says that we are to submit ourselves to God. When we do that, we can expect the promise to come to pass.

All prophecy is conditional whether conditions are stated or not. Unspoken conditions include: testing the prophetic word, writing the word on paper, walking in faith, waging warfare, being obedient to do what God has instructed, and having revelation that, even though we might feel that the word could never come to pass in our life, God is able to perform what He has promised to us.

Prophecies do not come to pass for various reasons. It could possibly not be a Word from God. On the other hand, it could be a Word from the Lord, but due to disobedience, it isn't fulfilled. Many times after a prophecy is received, it seems like the very next day the recipient's life goes totally in the opposite direction. A prophetic word is a Word from God. If it is not , we have no business messing with it. If it is, just as Satan comes immediately to steal the Word when it is ministered to us, so he will also attempt to steal the prophetic word. Satan does not want us to receive the blessings of God. God has given us an antidote for such a situation. It is found in 1 Tim. 1:18 - "This charge I commit unto thee, son Timothy, according to the prophecies which went before on thee, that thou by them mightiest war a good warfare. The weapons of our warfare are not carnal, but they are mighty through God to the tearing down of strongholds." As Satan attempts to lie to us regarding the prophetic word, we can take up that very prophecy, and wield it as a mighty weapon against him. If we have tested the prophecy, and it is affirmative in our testing, then we can use the prophecy as a weapon.

Tell the devil he's a liar, and the father of

---

lies. Read him the riot act by confessing your prophecy with your mouth.

Chapter Five

God's Method of Fulfilling Prophecy

Many people have made extreme mistakes in trying to take the role of God with regard to their prophecy. There are many things that have to be worked through before a prophecy will come to pass. Timing is one important factor. Often when we are under a large amount of stress we feel that we know better than God and cannot understand why He takes so long to answer our cry. This can result in feelings of rejection, thinking that God is not concerned and is not hearing our prayers. We feel that if He does not come through for us by a given time period we will be doomed, and in our dilemma we let God know that it's now time for Him to do something drastic. More often than not, our time frame does not fit in with God's and we seem to have to wait a bit longer for the answer than we thought was necessary. One reason for this is that time produces maturity in our lives. God has promised that He will not allow us to be tempted with more than we can endure and with each temptation He promises to make a way of escape. As we keep trusting Him and believing that He is faithfull to His promises even though the circumstances are desperate, God's character is perfected in our lives. God has a time period for everything and His timing is always perfect. He is never too early, and never too late. He is always on time.

For many years before Jesus came as Messiah to this earth, the Jews were earnestly seeking His coming, realizing the need for such an event in the world. I could imagine that many prayed instructing God just how much this world needed a Messiah. No amount of prayer could change God's timing. Galatians 4:4 says that in due time Christ died for the ungodly. The book of Ecclesiastes states that there is a time and a season for everything. As we look at situations in our lives, we may feel God has forgotten us, but we need to remember that there is a time and a season for everything. I have personally heard preachers say that is the Body of Christ would only do certain things, Jesus Christ would return. The same preachers claim that if we do not do these things we will delay the imminent return of the Lord. Nothing that we do can hasten or delay Christ's return. Jesus Himself said that the Father knows the day and the hour of Christ's return to the earth. That time is established in God's timetable and cannot be changed. It is an appointed time. Christ's return will not be because of us, but rather in spite of us.

As believers we will go through trials and hardships. Paul encouraged Timothy to be a good soldier of the Lord Jesus Christ. We do experience valley and mountain top situations in our life. Every believer who has been around for a while will have to agree that they have had valley as well as mountain top experiences. As we arrive on the top of the mountain we begin to enjoy the pleasures that we find there. Soon after arriving on our mountain top, the Lord asks whether we are enjoying the new experience of blessing and victory. Our answers are always affirmative. "Yes Lord, I really am enjoying this wonderful sunshine experience." No sooner have we answered when God will ask us to take a look ahead and explain what we see. As we look, we see another mountain ahead, only with one major difference; the mountain ahead is much higher than the one we are on. God then challenges us with the desire to move to the top of the mountain we see ahead. Any Christian who wants to go on with God will definitely answer with a loud YES. We then get the alarming news: THE ONLY WAY TO THE TOP OF THE NEXT MOUNTAIN IS THROUGH THE VALLEY THAT SEPARATES THEM. The only problem is that God has no airline services nor bridges that join the two mountains. There is only one way to the next mountain and that is through the valley. David said that it was in the valley that Christ restores us. Valley experiences do not have to be all negative, rather they can be extremely postive and can help us grow.

As I was praying about this one day (mainly because the idea went totally against my doctrine and theology), I asked God why so many christians live their lives in the valleys. The Lord answered almost immediately and said that it was because they did not realize that you only need to remain in the valley for as long as you choose. His Word is packed with the answers to victory and as we take the Word, while in the valley, and wield it as a mighty sword against the onslaught of the enemy, we would obtain the victory. Valley experiences are learning opportunities. The quicker we are willing to learn, the sooner we arrive at the top of the mountain. The choice is up to us. As I received revelation of this, when I now head into the valley, I cry to the Lord to help me be a quick learner. Each time I reach out to His Word in a greater measure and stand on the promises of God. Each time my valley experience has been a short and pleasant one. It did take some time for this to become a reality, but once I grasped the truth of this fact, each experience was sweet. Jesus promised that He would never leave us or forsake us.

The same thing is true with regard to our prophecies. To think that prophecy is automatic and is going to come to pass immediately is living in a fool's paradise. Nothing in God's Kingdom is automatic. Most prophetic words will take time to mature before it becomes a reality in our lives. A person who receives a word that they are going to have a world wide ministry can be sure that God is going to do a lot of His workings in their lives before the ministry materializes. God works more on the man than He does on the ministry. When God initially called Moses to be His man to lead the Israelites out of the land of Egypt, God first took Moses and placed him in the School of the Holy Ghost for a period of forty years. The reason for this was because God had to first get Moses out of Moses before Moses would be able to lead the Israelites out of Egypt. God worked on the man Jesus for thirty years before He released Him into ministry. It is interesting to note that Jesus only actively ministered for three and a half years. Ten years of training were invested into Christ's life for each year of ministry. Now, we do not want to build a doctrine around that, but rather note a principle. When a man's ministry grows bigger than the man, destruction of one kind or another is sure to take place. Many great men of God who have been our predecessors fell into this very trap of the enemy and although God used them mightily, toward the end of their lives they were led astray into some devastating area of deception. Although you might feel that God or man is taking rather long to recognize the gift and calling in your life, remember Jesus said that He would build His church. It does not matter what man might attempt to do, Jesus is going to get the job done. The Word also admonishes us that unless the Lord builds the house, those that labor, labor in vain. (PS. 127:1)

God promised Israel that He would lead them out of captivity into a land flowing with milk and honey. Not one part of that prophecy just fell into place overnight. Rather, Israel faced many obstacles, harships and battles as they journeyed from the prophecy to the promise. They had to face the torments of their pursuers, the temptations of unbelief, the strains of the desert, the boredom of the same food provision for forty years, the frustration of wandering, the loss of their leader, the crossing of the raging Jordan, the giants, wars and walled cities. It was no easy task. Yet, some kept holding onto the promise that God had given them and eventually after many ups and downs, possessed the prophetic promise. Even after receiving what God had prophetically spoken to them, they were still faced with many obstacles which they had to overcome.

An attitude regarding prophecy which says that if the prophecy comes to pass it is God, if it does not, then the word is not from God, is one that displays a true lack of knowledge. In Hosea, God said that His people perish because of the lack of knowledge. We have to realize that there is a timing and we need to pray and seek God to assist us in resting in Him until the fulfillment of His promise.

Even words that are spoken in prophecy which we interpret may not have the same interpretation with God. As the prophetic word is given, it is established in God's realm immediately, but can take time before it manifests in our realm. In 1 Sam. 13:14 the prophet Samuel prophesied God's judgement to King Saul and said, "Now your kingdom shall not continue...". As we read the scripture we would interpret that at that moment Saul's kingdom was over. In God's realm that fact was established at that moment, but it took almost forty years before the prophecy was fulfilled. As the prophetic word is brought to us, God's plan is revealed. It then can and many times does take a great while before we are ready to experience the fruit of the prophecy.

Chapter Six

Resurrecting That Tombed Prophecy

There are many reasons people lose the prophetic promise. The Israelites lost theirs because of unbelief and wandered in the wilderness for forty years. Many of them never obtained the promise God had made them. Moses was disobedient to God and instead of speaking to the rock to bring forth water, he smote the rock in anger. Water still gushed from the rock, but because of his disobedience to God, he was never allowed to possess the prophetic promise and enter the Promised Land. These, as well as a lack of knowledge, can be factors today that will hinder our prophetic promise becoming a reality in our lives. We might be at a point where we feel that the word that was spoken over us is embalmed and entombed and therefore will never become a reality. The good news is that Jesus and you can resurrect your prophetic word now. If you have put it to the test as discussed earlier in this book and found it to line up with God's order, even though it looks like it is dead and buried, rise up and possess the promise God has spoken to your heart.

When Jesus was called to assist His friend, Lazarus who was sick unto death, He did not drop everything and rush to his aid. Instead, He kept doing what He was doing and only arrived to assist Lazarus four days after he had died. By this time Lazarus had been embalmed and buried, but this did not deter the Lord. Everybody was upset and could not understand why Jesus had taken so long to come to the aid of a good friend. At a moment when everything seemed to be lost, Jesus Christ reached into the eternal realm of God and said, "Lazarus, come forth!" No angel in heaven nor demon in hell could hold him back. Life came back into Lazarus' lifeless body and before everybody, he walked out of the tomb. Nothing can hold back an authoritative Word of God. Maybe today it seems like your prophetic promise is embalmed and secured in it's tomb of doubt and unbelief. It is time to speak the authoritive Word of God and call it back into the realm of reality. Let me pray this prayer with you:

Father, I come to you today in the mighty name of Jesus. Lord, I believe that you have spoken a prophetic promise to me, but for some reason I have let go of that word. Today, I speak to that word and declare that you come forth in the name of Jesus. Lord, I thank you that you give me new hope this day and I believe that because this is a word from you, you are watching over it to perform it. I confess any doubt or unbelief I have harbored in this area and believe that you cleanse me from it. Thank you for bringing that revealed word back to me, causing it to have life. It now belongs to me. AMEN.

Now lets summarize the important aspects of your prophecy from beginning to end.

1. Receive the prophetic word without placing your own conditions on the word. Our conditions include requiring the word to declare what we wish. God does not always speak into every situation we want Him to. Silence does not mean that God is not interested in that given situation.

2. It is important to record the prophecy. The safe-

---

guard of recording the word helps us see the promises as well as the conditions. It also helps us not state things that were never mentioned in the prophetic word. Recording the prophecy should be on audio tape as well as written down.

3. Judge or test your prophecy with the fourfold test found in chapter four. Make sure it was a word from God. Highlight the noted conditions.

4. Be sure to fulfill ALL conditions.

5. Underline all the promises and hold fast to them. Remember, circumstances are the chief thieves of prophetic promises.

6. Walk in faith and obedience. Remember there is always a timing in all prophecy.

7. If there is a strain on the fulfillment of your prophecy, wage warfare according to 1 Tim. 1:18.

8. Meditate on the prophetic promise. Meditate means to continually say, to speak it over and over.

9. Wait patiently for the fulfillment of God's promise. Don't get anxious.

10. Remember, God is not a man that He should lie. His promises are yea and amen.

Chapter Seven

Guarding Your
Prophetic Promise

Once the prophetic promise has been received it needs to be guarded, because circumstances
of life will steal the word. The following is a guide-
line to help keep the promise before you:

1. Write the prophetic promise down. Hab. 2:2 says
to "Write the vision, and make it plain upon tables,
that he may run that readeth it." Writing the vision
helps to keep the vision before you. When it is written put it in a place where you will be able to read it
on a regular basis. Habakkuk promises that the vision will surely come to pass, it will not tarry. Keep-
ing the vision before you helps to keep the promise
fresh in your mind. It also assists in realizing that

there are conditions to the promise and that in order to obtain the promise, we need to fulfill the conditions. Unfulfilled conditions will result in unfulfilled promises. In James 4:7 God gives us a promise that if we resist the devil he will flee from us. The promise is great, but will not work unless we fulfill the condition which is found in the same verse, namely; "Submit yourself unto God." Unless we fulfill the condition, the promise is null and void. When prophecy is spoken over our lives, as human beings we tend to grasp the highlights or promises of the prophecy and seldom remember the conditions God might include. As we write the prophetic word down on paper, we begin to see the full extent of what God is saying; conditions as well as promises.

2. Keep on watering your prophecy with the utterance of your mouth. Matt. 12:37 says that "for by your words you shall be justified and by your words you shall be condemned." This is not a name it, claim it and frame it doctrine. I believe the church has gone way beyond that point and has matured in some of its weird beliefs it conjured with this regards. Rather, this is giving spiritual water to the word God has given you and will cause that word to become rhema or revelation knowledge. Once your prophetic word is revelation knowledge, there

is nothing in this world that can steal it from you, as at that point you know that you know that you know God has spoken it to you. Watering your prophetic word by the confession of your mouth causes that word to become established in your heart. Speak the Word of God over your prophetic word and let it take root.

ABOUT THE AUTHOR

Kevin van der Westhuizen was born and raised in South Africa. Since 1979 Kevin has worked in full-time ministry. During this time he founded two churches, and also established the first Christian non-racial school in the city of Alberton, South Africa.

God called Kevin into full-time Prophetic Ministry in May 1989 at which time he resigned as Senior Pastor to respond to the call to the nations.

Kevin has a desire to see Prophetic Ministry flowing in the church in truth and sincerity. He travels with his wife, Loreen, and two children, Janice and Glenn.

God has allowed him to visit 26 nations on 3 continents. Kevin travels world-wide conducting Schools of the Prophetic Seminars in various churches.

He also heads the School of the Prophetic in Colorado U.S.A.